The Daughter Left Behind: Navigating Life Without My Mother
By Danielle Moore

ISBN: 979-8-218-41786-4

This book is dedicated to a future, healed me and you.

WE will be ok and you are not alone.

I love you.

Foreword

Born from the deep sense of loss after her Mother's departure, this narrative unveils the resilience of the human spirit and the unexpected strength found within. "The Daughter Left Behind" is an intimate exploration into a young woman's journey, navigating grief, resilience, and the enduring power of love through the complexities of grief that arise from embracing loss.

As my stepdaughter shares her deeply personal journey, readers are invited into a realm of raw emotion, vulnerability, and a celebration of the unwavering human spirit.

May "The Daughter Left Behind" serve as a source of solace and understanding for those who tread the path of grief. In immersing yourself in the author's journey, you will witness the beauty that emerges from the ashes of sorrow—a testament to the enduring nature of love and the profound legacy a mother leaves behind.

Through the author's introspective lens, we gain insight into the impact a mother's presence, even in her absence, can have on her daughter's life.

To Danielle,

In the delicate tapestry of life, threads woven by fate intertwine to shape our journey, we've forged a connection that surpasses biology. You're gonna be just fine, Little One. I love you,

Alice Moore

Chapter I

" Carla Ruth Gage, 42, of Beaumont, Texas. Died Monday, January 14, 2008 at Christus St. Elizabeth Hospital. Funeral will be Saturday, January 26, 2008, at 11:00 am at Antioch Missionary Baptist Church with burial at Sacred Heart Cemetery under the direction of Calvary Mortuary staff. Visitation will be from 9:00 am to 11:00 am Saturday at the church. Survivors include her father, Raymond Gage Jr. of Beaumont, Texas, son Nathan D. Moore and daughter, Danielle N. Moore of Beaumont, Texas. Sisters Sheyle Henton, Charlotte Gage, Sheryl Gage of Beaumont, Texas and Rachel Gage of Houston, Texas; brothers, Raymond Gage III and Alexander Chambers-Gage of Beaumont, Texas, and a host of other relatives and friends".

read the obituary of my mother. My life changed in a matter of hours, little did I know that morning I got up and was ready for school. How was I supposed to know that by the end of that day, I would be changed for the rest of my life?

January 14, 2008, after weeks of getting chewed out for failing math I was finally passing. I'd gotten an eighty-nine on a test which pulled my average up to a seventy if I remember correctly, (reaching for the stars I know). But, that was huge for me, math has always been a struggle. I even asked to bring it home so I could show my mom. My grandpa picked my brother and me up after school, though not the routine, it wasn't completely uncommon.

Upon getting into the car I ask, "Where's mom?".

I'm told that she is in the hospital. We'll go see her later in the day. Again, it's not uncommon, my family is relatively sickly so that wasn't out of the ordinary. I thought nothing of it, if anything my good grade and the fact that I was passing will make her feel better. Nonetheless, we carry on about our day; we go home, do our homework, eat dinner and finally, it's time to go see mom.

Once there I noticed that most of my family was there. It didn't hit me that this could mean my mom isn't doing well, I was just happy to see them. At one point I forget we're even in a hospital. There were jokes going around between everyone. We were playing in the section we had and everything. There wasn't a feeling of death in the air honestly. I remember feeling happy to see everybody. I remember thinking my mom was going to feel so much love from having everyone be there. Having laughed so much I'd forgotten why I was even there. The feeling of love and family was heavy, I couldn't wait for my mom to feel that everyone was there for her. I remember telling stories of us all. Looking back on it, I should've known something was wrong. I should've known she wasn't ok. Otherwise, why would everybody be here? Why would family from out of town have come to see my mom if she was ok and going to be coming home soon?

Then, the atmosphere changed. I felt it as soon as it happened. My aunt, her sister, is such a gentle person but, at this moment I didn't want her near me. Before this moment my aunt and I weren't close by any means. For the first time, I think I'm actually seeing her. She walks over to us (my brother and I) in what feels like slow motion. I knew what she would say before the words left her mouth.

Grabbing both of our hands and walking us to an empty part of the hallway she says, "I'm sorry baby but your mom passed". She has tears in her eyes and I want her to repeat herself even though I know what she said won't change. I don't believe her at first even as I crumble to the ground. For the first time, I feel alone. The hallway fades and I don't see or hear anything around me. I see that she's still talking and somebody is trying to hold me up. Finally, the sound comes back to me and all I hear is screaming. I remember wondering who was screaming and wanting them to shut up.

Minutes pass before I realize it's me that's screaming but I can't stop it. The lights seem so dark now. Everything seems so dull. Why can't I stop screaming? My aunt tries to soothe me to no avail.

"NO, NO, NO, NO!", I scream repeatedly. Thinking not her. My mom can't be dead. Moms aren't supposed to die. Why am I being punished?

I was thirteen when my life changed. Walking slowly to her room to see her didn't seem real. None of this seemed real. Seeing her with tubes coming out of her mouth and machines beeping didn't seem like it was real. She didn't even look like herself. Still crying but quietly now, I think that's the moment I decided to only let myself hear my cries seeing as the only person that would care about them is dead. She looked so bloated then, now I've learned that's what bodies do after death. Time stood still and I felt as if I weren't breathing. Almost like I wasn't there really. At the same time, she looked so peaceful like she was sleeping. I know she wasn't but, I think I told myself that she was asleep. I told myself that she'd wake up any moment even though I knew in the back of my mind that she wouldn't. I loved that woman with all that I had at age thirteen but I hadn't realized that until then. Until I saw her then I didn't know how much she meant to me. I hadn't known just how much she was my world. Funny how that happens right? It's funny how we don't think of those things on a day-to-day basis, we just carry on about our lives, almost in a dream right?

But this woman that's lying in this bed. My WORLD is lying in this bed, her soul gone but her body still here. Her body lay so comfortably; no more worries, no more cares. I shut off at that moment. Feeling nothing and only seeing her. Seeing every wrongdoing I've done. I instantly remember the time I made her cry and every fight we ever had. I remember every time I snuck out, every time I screamed hateful things to her. My one true love was no more and my brain can't take it. I feel my brain breaking as I scream once more.

Hands grab me and pull me out of the room. I fight them off because what else am I to do? How dare you pull me away from my love? HOW DARE YOU pull me away from the one person who understands me? The one person who saw me, who cared. The one person who cared if I lived or died. The one person who would truly feel if I were to leave this world. How dare these hands pull me away from her? At that moment I changed yet again. Isn't that funny? I could almost laugh thinking back on everything. Moments change us in an instant. We don't even know what those moments are or when they will happen, as they happen. Goodness, I felt this change as it happened though. I felt myself breaking and suddenly becoming warm after what felt like years though it had been only hours. How dare you leave me mother?

"Grief is like living two lives. One is where you pretend that everything is alright. The other is where your heart screams silently in pain."

-Unknown

Chapter II

Of course, I'm hurting. I mean who wouldn't be? My mom just died and I don't really know which way is up. A lot of tears and whatnot, plans for the funeral. At least that's how I assume a kid who just lost her mom would be feeling. I, on the other hand, felt a numbing heat.

That heat was hatred. For my mom, for God, for the whole damned world. Because I was left alone, who was going to teach me stuff now? Who would be my forever friend? I remember thinking these things off and on throughout the years. I didn't know what healing was. I didn't know that there are things in your life you need to heal from to be a better person.

I remember getting my hair braided for her funeral. This one small thing I used to look forward to and loved getting done by my mom was now a chore. I remember going to the lady's house and her braiding my hair into a ponytail. Cornrows were once my favorite hairstyle, now it just seemed like part of the costume I wore as the grieving daughter.

I can't even tell you what I wore other than it was a dress, most likely black, along with stockings and maybe a sweater. It seemed like a lifetime had passed by when I finally saw her again. But I can't lie to you and say I remember what she looked like in that casket. Praying that it was some sick joke and she was just sleeping and she'd wake up any minute now. I'm not entirely sure when it hit me that it wasn't a joke and she wasn't sleeping.

I was inconsolable. At some point, I started screaming again. I remember being walked out to the hallway and not wanting anybody to touch me but my dad. I screamed for my dad like a newborn baby taking their first breath in this world, I wouldn't let anyone touch me. I mean my fucking mom just died. How can you soothe that ache?

The craziest thing was I wasn't even surprised that he, my dad, was there. I think it would've surprised me more if he wasn't. But, he was here, and I felt loved once more. □Is that crazy? I've seen this man, all of MAYBE 3 or 4 times in my entire life and just him being here made me feel loved again. Could it have been because he's my surviving parent? To this day I'm not sure.□ My amazing dad who smelled like he'd poured a whole bottle of liquor on his person was here and I was safe, again. I curled up in his lap and cried myself to sleep while he rubbed my back. I will admit at first I played possum. I'd gotten very good at it by this time. I learned if I just lie still enough with my eyes closed people won't try to talk to me. And I was a grieving kid so nobody would bother me.

I remember somebody, maybe my aunt, asking my dad something or telling him something and he responded with, “Nah, she's good.” That short sentence made me feel like I would be ok. For just a second the hatred left me. Sitting on my dad’s lap at my mom’s funeral I felt protected. I felt saved from this dark hole I was slowly falling down. As I sat in my father's arms my hatred for my mother grew. Because, how unthoughtful was she to get sick and leave her kids? Her family?

We just kind of deal with it, not really understanding, and in turn, drawing our own conclusions from situations. I didn’t know my parents' situation nor was it ever discussed with me. Then, I thought my father just didn’t want to be a father. Now, I understand that it doesn’t always work out with parents.

I wish I could say looking back now I see everything clearer. But, that’s not the case with this. Most of the middle I remember in pieces. As if it was from a movie I’d seen many many years ago. I do however remember “meeting” my dad. I put that in quotations because I'd met him before, obviously, and definitely knew who he was. His role was fairly nonexistent to me though, for whatever reason. Funny things happen between parents and us kids.

It had been told to me before that my dad was going to come and take us. I remember stressing over this, because how can this be true? I don't even really know dude like that. He doesn't even know us. How is he just going to come and "take us"? Who tf he think he is? All of these things are going through my head.

I'm then told I have to make a very important decision. It was my choice to say if we stayed with my mom's family or went with my dad. Ok, firstly, I was a child and shouldn't have been given that decision to make. I believe a kids' feelings are important in relation to where they stay. BUT, that is a serious and very important decision to make. My mind was not developed enough to make the RIGHT decision for our future and the betterment of us. Our feelings should have been put into consideration but that's a lot to put on a kid.

NOW, sitting in the living room of my grandparent's home staring at this stranger, I look so much like. I try to find pieces of myself in his appearance. Having only seen him maybe a handful of times. I am numb.

Even though a small part of me prayed for our dad to take us out of this, I knew I couldn't leave my brother. And, he most definitely didn't want to go. Now I had the duty of taking care of my brother. No one put this on me but no one took it off of me either. So... I made the decision to stay.

I feel like I've paid for that decision in the years that followed. My family was dead as far as I was concerned. My mom had died though I didn't know it then, she was my world. Since she left the rest of my family did too. By the end of that same year, the only other man who was very instrumental in my life, my grandpa, died as well. So what would I care about now?

I looked at this man with annoyance on my face but pleading in my eyes, and he didn't see it. How could he not see that I was pleading for him to save me? How can he call himself a parent if he couldn't see that? For that, I decided he didn't possibly want us or care for us. I decided I hated him. This was the start of a complex I'd struggle with for the rest of my life. Feelings of being forgotten or being unimportant when a person I care about doesn't "see" something I'm pleading for. Though I wouldn't make it vocal.

“Some people will expect you to heal alone, immediately. Some will support you, for a while. And some will stay by your side, a lighthouse in your storm, constant and steady. The hard part is, you don’t get to choose which one you get. And sometimes, you won’t get anyone at all.”

- ***Julie Anne Addicott***

Chapter III

Middle school was hard after that. I stayed in cheerleading but I hated it now. I only joined because my mom wanted me to cheer and she was so happy about it. She brought me something to eat after every practice and never missed a game I cheered at. Now that she is gone I can't quit now. Even though I was an asshole through most practices and got demerits left and right, for any and everything. Most days I couldn't even make it through the day at school. Sometimes I could start to cry in the middle of class. There were times when I would run out of class to the restroom because being around people was just too much. By this time I'd started self-harming myself in the form of starvation and cutting. To this day I struggle with both.

Throughout my eighth grade year, I had a few

teachers that understood and cared. They tried at least. I had a few that noticed the cuts and some almost got through to me. But, this was the only thing I could control. I felt so ashamed about it. I remember one teacher in particular, Coach Walker, he'd noticed my change in attitude and he noticed some cuts on my arm one day when my jacket sleeve rose up. He took me out into the hallway and told me he saw me. He said, " I'm sure it's been really hard for you since you lost your mom. But, don't forget how beautiful and smart you are. And I'm sure your mom wouldn't want you doing this to yourself. If you ever need to talk I'll listen." I was so far from caring about what this man was saying to me. I didn't necessarily hear the words he said; I heard how he said them. He was calm and nice. He didn't talk to me like I was stupid or scream at me with anger. It was his tone that made me listen. He made sure to include me in classroom discussions and didn't let me simply fall through the cracks and be overlooked. I think of him silently every now and again. Thank you Coach Walker for speaking to me gently and with care in that hallway in eighth grade.

I was ashamed that I was cutting though. It was my dirty little secret. To the point that I wore Jean pants and jackets or hoodies year around. It didn't matter how hot it got outside, I would not be without a jacket of some kind. My family never really questioned it at this time. I didn't know how bad it would be when they did find out.

I honestly don't remember when my family found out about the cutting. And honestly, they didn't react like they were concerned or even cared. They reacted like I'd inconvenienced them with my declining mental state. When my uncle found out he was livid. I still remember standing outside with him sitting in his car in front of my grandparents' house. He's asking me why I was cutting myself and I knew I couldn't give him an answer he would accept. Because the answer was it felt good to feel something. It felt good to be able to physically see the pain and anger I felt run out of me in the form of my blood. As I'm thinking of all of this I'm snapped back to reality by his shouts and meet him with a small "I don't know", and a shrug of the shoulders.

My uncle then goes on to say, "Since you like to be cut go get me one I'll cut you too." To that, I start to cry because who says this shit to a teenager that's barely hanging on. To my resounding "No"

He replied with, " You don't care about getting infected or catching gangrene. So why should I care? You're being stupid I want to be stupid too."

He told me to stop doing that and stop being stupid. You would think it'd stop at the adults right? The adults that wanted me. The adults that were supposed to be watching me and raising me. But nope, my cousins found out too.

From them, I was graced with the nickname the butcher. Not just from them but an aunt of mine thought it was a good idea to play along calling me this. I was asked, “What’s on the menu today?”

I didn’t know how to vocalize the control I felt when I tried to get a release of the emotions I was feeling. At times I would feel so much physically crippling pain. Now I see it and understand it as I have an addiction that I live with every single day. Nothing too different from an alcoholic or drug addict. Maybe others would think differently but it has been a coping mechanism. I would continue to struggle with this horrible coping mechanism for years to come.

To say I felt like shit would be putting it mildly. My brother and I were brought to a cousin's house so that my brother “could get a good talking to”. That little intervention I guess was really just our older cousin telling us how much of a nuisance we were.

To say I wanted to be done with all of these people isn't even the start of it. We were told we were the reason our mother died over and over through the years by multiple family members. That we were so stressful and troublesome that she died. We were told we wouldn't get the chance to kill our nanny or anybody else in the family. At the time I didn't understand that this was all traumatic. So what did the family do? If you said "ignored us" you'd be correct. They ignored us or treated us like we were the most inconvenient thing for them to deal with like a road being closed on their route of life. All of them except our nanny Toots. She really did try to give us the love we were missing.

I already felt abandoned by my dad's side; I didn't know I was being kept away from them for whatever reason. I felt abandoned by my dad; thinking because I chose to stay he didn't want me anymore. Now, I felt I was being abandoned by my mom's side. The only difference is that I chose to be here. I chose the hell I was living thinking versus going to the unknown. Maybe if I had known my dad better I might've made a different decision. Though I try not to live in the world of what-ifs, my mind wanders from time to time.

Nobody noticed I rarely ate, and what I did eat in front of them I took laxatives shortly after to purge it out of me. I had also moved to cutting my thighs since my nanny and family had caught on to my arm. Sometime after, my nanny had had enough I guess. She threatened to search me every day like she had to do the patients at her job and take my door off the hinges. I wasn't allowed to use razors anymore BUT now I could use Nair for all of my body hair removal needs. I was taken to a therapist; and put on medication and that fixed everything, right? WRONG!

“Your heart doesn’t have a lot

of space these days, and the cloud

over your head just keeps getting

bigger.

Yet you show up.

You breathe in.

You hold on.

You pull through.”

Chapter IV

High school was a whole new animal. See when you don't actually get to the root of what's wrong you find other ways to cope. Nobody ever treated losing my mom so young as a traumatizing experience so I didn't know it was one for a very long time.

Everybody else went on with their life. The carousel never stopped turning for them and they expected it to be the same for us. We were never taught how to deal with the feelings that come with losing a parent. We were treated like orphans by everyone EXCEPT our nana. But what exactly could she TEACH us? She was dealing with a major loss as well. Who was going to teach us that we truly had our whole lives to live? How to actually be a part of a family? Or teach me the things I needed to know in order to be a well-rounded woman?

I had to figure this shit out myself. In hindsight, I'm sure I could've called our dad to come and get us, or at least get me. But, I really didn't even think that was an option, besides that, pride is a hell of a thing. Crazy thing now is I didn't even know what pride was then, at least not really. I didn't know how crippling it could be. Because of that, I decided I would raise Nathan and me. I mean who else was going to do it? Nobody really cared about us, nobody really saw us outside of being the orphan kids they were now responsible for.

Can a kid REALLY raise themself correctly, to be a decent part of society?

Honestly, I don't even remember much of freshman year. I remember being a part of the flag team. I had two very close friends and it was great. I also remember going to parties a lot, I started drinking around this time. There was also a lot of skipping school or leaving early during that time. Also, during this, I figured out how to feel again. I thought it was amazing, but I didn't realize that you give a piece of yourself to each partner you share your body with, no matter how you tell yourself it's just sex, nothing serious. Even though I wasn't a virgin sex was still a very new thing for me to be indulging in.

I never did hard drugs, only weed, and pretty heavily. (2 star rating. Would not recommend it, as it can cause numbing of emotions.) I learned that I finally could feel something during sex; if even for a second and, nothing at the same time. FINALLY, I felt like SOMEBODY wanted me. A boy is just glad to be getting in your pants. A boy is just glad to be getting some so they say the things that boys say to get in your pants. It's like they know how to weed out the girls that have low self-esteem. The girls that are falling through the cracks, the ones you don't really have to "convince" because everyone in their life has shown they don't give a damn or aren't worth the attention. And I was the poster child for low self-confidence. There are so many young girls in this world who feel so alone and don't have anybody looking out for them. So they, like myself, hold on to any small form of companionship. There are so many girls that just want to be truly unconditionally loved, seen, and accepted. So, when a boy says he loves you or that he will be there for you and you don’t have that coming from anywhere else you believe him. Even though I know now just how wrong I was. I wish so badly I could go back and hug the younger me. Talk to her to get her to understand her worth. I wish I could get her to let go of the anger and worthlessness she felt in the world. I wish so desperately I could hold her and tell her the love she’s searching for comes from her, not others. That she is beautiful and smart, she just needs to apply herself. I would also try convincing her that she’s not fat no matter what she’s told. I would tell my younger self “I love you, I need you, you deserve to love and be loved correctly. It is ok to have emotions and show them, BUT don't let them rule your life, love. You are powerful beyond your knowledge".

Summer before tenth grade I went to live with my uncle (my mom's brother) and his wife in Atlanta, Georgia. I wasn't sent to live there or anything I initially went just for the summer. I had tons of fun actually though my uncle was kind of strict. It was a good change of pace and environment. My aunt didn't have any kids so it was fun to pretend she was my mom. We'd go get our hair done together and go shopping. It was really nice, I even "worked" with her a bit during the summer.

As the end of summer rolled around my nanny came for a visit and to bring me back to Beaumont. I remember writing this two or three-page letter to my nanny. I don't remember verbatim what I wrote but I told her that I liked girls and I hoped she didn't hate me or think I was disgusting. I wrote saying I hope she still loved me and didn't disown me. That I didn't choose this and felt I was just trying to be true to myself. It was then that I decided to ask if I could stay for the upcoming school year. I'd already talked to my uncle and aunt about this and they were ok with it. She also was ok with it, and eventually, the needed paperwork was sent from Beaumont to Atlanta. I mean what could go wrong right?

At first, it was fantastic. I'd made friends in my building and had somebody to do homework with, it was great. My new school was huge and the people were different. From the way they talked to being from pretty much everywhere. I met a guy from New York, and yes he sounded very New York but he was really cool. There was a guy in my building from Ethiopia, we also went to the same school. I got to eat Ethiopian food one time when we were working on a project together and man oh man was it good. I experienced so many different foods in Atlanta.

It was like a mixing pot of different cultures, it was exhilarating.

Once school started I eventually found a small group of friends. My small group consisted of Jordan who was a year younger than me and my neighbor. Also, Melissa, Taylor, Derrick. The three of us were inseparable during the time that school was in session. We ate lunch together and hung out between classes. It was great and I felt so accepted. Only during school though because my family didn't know their family; if you come from a black family you know EXACTLY what I mean. During school though I was in what seemed like a perfect world.

I noticed how ok everybody was "being themselves". I shortly started to get really comfortable with being myself too... only at school though. I'd come out to my aunt and uncle only to be met with disgust. They didn't say it out loud but by then I'd gotten pretty good at deciphering the underlying meaning of what people actually mean. I'm usually right by the way.

I would struggle with sexuality; whether it was right or wrong, whether I was a good person. At some part of this year, I got a girlfriend. I loved her, at least at the time I thought I did. Long distance isn't a problem for two sixteen-year-olds because we have love and trust, right? I threw myself into this all-consuming relationship. We talked about marriage and kids. Kid names and where we'd move, it was beautiful. I truly thought it would be forever because who would talk about these things if they weren't serious?

I can feel you rolling your eyes. But, it's the truth I just knew we were going to be together forever. Who was I to question what we had? I just knew in my soul my Prince Charming was actually a Princess Charming. And I loved her until we loved others. We agreed to be friends and that was that. My next girlfriend loved me just as consumingly.

Calling DeKalb County my home is crazy, right? Remember that huge decision I made last year about staying with my brother? Yet, here we were separated a year and a half later. These adults are still letting me, now 15 years old, decide where I live. My dad was back home in Beaumont at this time. I would later learn that he didn't know about us moving. He had let us go because we were going to stay together and, here we were living in two different states.

Atlanta was a freaking life experience. I'm so glad I got to experience it. I mean I was living my BEST LIFE. I went to work with my aunt every day that summer. I had 'money of my own'. It was great, it was perfect. Everything was perfect, until it wasn't.

"Not everyone is suffering loudly.

But we are all in pain.

So bea little more kind towards the quiet ones.

For their pain has no sound."

-Swati Bari

Chapter V

Still I ended up feeling wrong, there was a moment during school where I was told I just needed a “real” man to show me I wasn’t really gay. I was pushed against lockers ever so often. Slowly I became afraid of boys/men. I remember one night being at one of my aunt’s boyfriend's house to spend the night. Why this was ok I had no idea but it happened. My aunt and cousins were there as well but still. Anyway this particular night the kids stayed up. One by one we each fell asleep until it was only the boyfriend’s son, we’ll call him Brandon, and myself left up. I thought we were just shooting the shit, you know? Eventually, Brandon had questions about why I was gay. To which I kept it short and sweet by saying, “I just prefer girls”. Like every boy our age, he stated I just needed a man to fuck me one good time and I’d see I wasn't gay.

Why do boys/men think this is the answer? Sir, I don't want you or anyone else of your gender for that matter. Why is it taken so personally? Not once have I heard of a guy saying he's gay and a girl/woman taking time from her life to tell him you just haven't had the right vagina. Like really, get over yourself.

Somewhere in between me laughing him off and commenting on just how good I was on that act, his hands found their way into my shorts. I'm sure you're probably thinking how did we get here? Honestly, your guess is as good as mine because I have no clue. Right as I'm saying 'What the fuck' his hand starts to move inside my sleeper shorts. My mouth is telling him to stop while trying to jump down off the washing machine and his mouth finds its way to mine. I am disgusted, to say the least. His mouth moves away from mine as I am now pinned against the washer I was just sitting on top of. I remember hearing him tell me how good I should feel now that a real man had his hands on me. I look up at his face and I'm met with a smile on his lips and clear lust in his eyes. I start to feel tears come down my face, I don't even remember starting to cry. Seeing my tears he looks confused now.

“Shit”, he says and starts to push me away while pulling his hand out of my shorts. This boy whom I'd only known for all of two days had just assaulted me in the blink of an eye and I hadn't even known it really.

As soon as he stepped away from me I ran to the room where all the girls were sleeping as quickly and quietly as I could. Quietly cried myself to sleep while simultaneously soothing myself. I'd just about perfected the art of silent crying by this time. I prayed that my girlfriend would come and rescue me. I told myself I was ok, that everything was alright. A part of me was also scolding myself. Wondering if it was my fault that happened. If I hadn't laughed with him as much or been up so late. If I hadn't been so nice none of this would've happened. Though none of this was true. I was not ok and everything was not alright and it's not my fault. I was assaulted. I should've told somebody. But I never did, who would believe me? I went over everything in my head for the next 6 days after that. I wondered did I give even the slightest inkling that I was attracted to him? Should I have worn pants instead to bed? Should I not have talked to him at all? Should I have gone to bed when everybody else did? I learned from that experience. It would take another year and some change for me to let a boy touch me again. But it would take another eleven years for me to be comfortable with it.

Eventually, I started stealing liquor from the liquor cabinet at home (such a cliche I know). I would pour it in empty water bottles straight sometimes or mix it with a bit of some kind of juice on the way to school. Nobody noticed anything different. I started lying about my whereabouts and sneaking out. I started sneaking my girlfriend into our complex when I was supposed to be babysitting my cousins. Life started to be 'not so perfect'. Eventually, I was shipped back to live with my nanny. The 10th grade year was something I'd never forget.

Whether you've just started your journey of healing or you've been on it for years. Never make yourself comfortable crying silently. ALWAYS tell when somebody has touched your body unwarranted, no matter who it is. Do not care how you will be perceived. You tell loudly and boldly to anyone who will listen. Do not chip away at yourself. Because all you're left with then is a hollow shell of who you were and who you should've been. Your voice matters. It mattered when it happened, it matters now and it will always matter. You are always valid love. So don't drown yourself in quietness, because that quietness can be deafening. Always lift your head.

"I will not apologize for my strength

and the way it intimidates you.

I will not tame my spirit and the way it howls.

I will not be less"

Chapter VI

I've been through boyfriends and girlfriends, situation-ships, the whole nine. Up until now, I've hated everything and everyone. God himself couldn't even be my friend on MySpace. Because you're ALL POWERFUL RIGHT? You could've taken anybody so why her? I had grown to hate the phrase, "God needed her back home. She's in a better place now", because motherfucker WHAT? How can he need her more than we did? He knew her already, we were just getting to know her. I was just getting to know her.

Looking back now I can honestly say I wish there had been somebody around at that time that helped me keep my relationship with God. I know, I know, very typical, right? But I really do, at some point I pulled into myself. No longer allowing myself to show excitement unapologetically and outloud. At some point I had changed and didn't even realize it. I remember not being afraid to be happy. Not being afraid of the decisions I was making. I wholeheartedly had faith in the world around me. Before my world was rocked I had faith that my world would always spin, that I would always have unending joy and contentment with my life. Up until the people I loved the most were taken from me I truly lived life every single day. I had faith in my beliefs and in the people I could trust. I don't remember the exact day but it changed. I no longer believed God wanted better for me. I no longer believed he cared for me. Isn't that crazy how in a snap that can happen? I wish there was someone understanding in my corner at that time that could have helped me remember I'm here for a reason, and God doesn't want to hurt me.

My mom's side of the family not really giving a shit about us kind of pushed me on this "journey" to find somebody to love me. I mean who was going to show me what love was? As far as I was concerned I had no mom, I had no dad, I barely had a brother, I had nobody. Feelings of worthlessness and guilt because why did my mom die when she had too much love and meaning in this world but I didn't?

I'd wish over and over again for God to take me and bring her back. Though I knew that wasn't a fair trade I know. But, what's the point of me being here still? Nobody needed me. Nobody really wanted me. All my life up until this point I've been Poppey's(my grandpa) baby. I'm the only girl of my mom's siblings and that title has never felt so worthless. I've loved being the only girl for thirteen years of my life. Even when I got in trouble for the most part I could always go to my grandpa. My mom would always make me feel special. It didn't matter who I was up against, my mom would ALWAYS fight for me.

I understand now that I took that for granted. But, that's what kids do, we take life for granted.

We think this will last forever. The long summer days of meeting up with friends having no plans or ways to make these plans happen. We just live life. I thought my family would always be my family. I knew my aunts, uncle and cousins treated me differently. I knew it was most likely because I was the only girl. I just didn't realize exactly what the word 'family' really meant. I hadn't realized my family really began and ended with my mom and grandpa.

I don't think anyone realizes family relationships have to be built, they aren't automatic. You have to learn how to be open with brothers, sisters, cousins and such. At the time in my life where these relationships are made stronger my 'relationships' were severed.

I'd spent my whole life thinking they didn't matter. That I was better off as the island I now was. Truth is I did need my family around me. I'd needed to be told I was loved and wanted. I'd needed to be shown that I was still special though my rock is gone. I'd needed to be shown that there was somebody in this world that would still fight for me.

In all honesty I shouldn't have given my nanny such a hard time. I know I was struggling and that's true, but I could've let up a bit. I love my nanny, she truly is a Godsend, and I thoroughly feel I'd be dead had she not stepped in. Thank you nanny.

"She changed,

but not overnight like in the books you read. Over years. Slowly and painfully. Sometimes brutally.

But she did."

Chapter VII

Now I am a teen mom.

In 11th grade, I met the other half of my soon-to-be family. We were together for a year before I got pregnant. Understand it's only been three years since we lost my mom. I struggled with that for about 2 weeks. I went through my options with myself before I ever talked to anybody.

First, my thought was to get an abortion, I mean how the hell was I going to raise a kid in high school with no job, no car, no support? Next, I thought of adoption because at least this baby would have a good life, a better life. But, then I had to think of the downsides to these things. First, abortion, I know the process of abortion in and out, though I'd never had one. I've done research and reports on it and the different types of abortions there are. But, I knew if I went through with it I'd hate myself. I knew I would feel like a murderer and I would never forgive myself for snuffing out this life that could've been a great artist or songwriter. I would've always felt like a killer and that would've killed me, I valued life too much.

Then, there was adoption, and though adoption sounds like a beautiful thing there are so many kids that don't get adopted. There are some kids that are adopted by monsters or put in a horrible foster home. Those kids are molested and treated horribly. I knew I wouldn't be able to live with myself if I let this kid, who's not even bigger than a tomato yet, go. Upon these thoughts and decisions I had to make I spoke to Olajawon, the father and my boyfriend at the time. I told him I was thinking about an abortion or adoption. To which I was met with the response, " If you kill or give away my baby I'm going to beat your ass." Now I don't know if buddy was serious or not but I took him at his word so the option I'm left with is to keep it and raise it.

After listening to Olajawon tell me how we are in this together, and that we're a family now. Listening to the many times he told me he wouldn't be like his father or mine, how he'd be there for our baby and we'd raise it together. At the words "family" and "together", I was in. Then I had the thought that this little human WILL love me. I'll be the best mom I can be and this little person will be mine. Finally, after searching for it in everybody else I'll have a family.

Telling my aunt was the scariest thing. Though I already knew I was pregnant having peed on 4 tests over the course of two weeks. I still wasn't sure though because these things can be wrong right? Even though I had already been through my options and I'd picked an option, I still tried to convince myself I wasn't. Funny right?

I thought she'd hate me. I thought she'd send me away to some school for pregnant girls when their families disowned them (I watched entirely too much TV). So I told her my stomach had been hurting. She took me to my pediatrician like any good parental guide would. Ok, let's pause again. ANYTIME you still have a pediatrician you most definitely should not be having sex. Anytime your doctor is a pedi-anything I need you to slow down my love. I needed more than anything for someone to see the road I was going down and tell me to slow down. Actually, I did have somebody tell me to slow down, my teachers at school, but I was so delirious I thought I had it all under control. They saw that I was spiraling and tried to talk to me, but I didn't listen. Listen, my love. Your life matters to somebody.

Ok back to the story... So my aunt made the appointment for us to go and I'm getting checked out. She asked me the questions all doctors ask us around the age of seventeen. “Are you having sex?” To that, I answer with a lying no. “Is there any chance you could be pregnant?” To this question, I just shrug my shoulders. If my aunt's eyes could pop out of her head they would’ve. But my doctor caught on to my discomfort and asked if I would like my aunt to step out of the room. I said yes please in the smallest voice I’ve heard from myself in some time. Again my aunt's eyes want to leave her face but she does as is asked. Once the door is closed again I tell my doctor maybe. STILL, I’m trying to convince myself the four pregnancy tests I peed on have lied.

My doctor tells me she’s going to send me to get a blood test. So she does the paperwork and tells my aunt she’s sending me to get some blood work done and off we go. We get to the place and I get the work done. I’ve sat in these people's faces knowing damned well I’m pregnant and I’m sitting here wasting everybody's time. The whole time I'm getting my blood drawn I'm thinking to myself just tell her. She is going to find out anyway when you get fat and a baby pops out of you! I finally told her though. ON THE WALK TO THE DAMNED CAR! In a small voice for the second time that day, I said "The reason we are here is because I'm pregnant." My aunt pauses and asks "What?" So I say again. "We're here because I'm pregnant." If looks could kill, I'd be dead.

My aunt isn't a mean person. Not once did she scream at me. But her silence was deafening. She didn't look mad either, just really disappointed. Very softly she tells me to get in the car. We drove off in silence back to the house.

Looking back on my and Olajawon relationship, we were never right for each other. He cheated on me for most of our relationship and then, ended up dumping me because I called a girl he was cheating on me with from his phone (rookie mistake). He said, "I can't be with somebody who doesn't trust me, and I don't trust anymore." (Ironic isn't it?) Sir, WHAT? How did you get to that conclusion? He came to that conclusion because he wanted to sleep around as much as he wanted without feeling guilty.

So I was a statistic all the way around. Except I didn't drop out of school. I waddled my butt to every class. I wore whatever fit me most days and threw up my breakfast by 11:30 am. I slept in most of my classes. My homeroom teacher actually caught on and I stopped getting in trouble for falling asleep in her class. I would have breakfast in her class most mornings. She'd make me apple cinnamon oatmeal with raisins and that helped me not throw up by midday. It also gave me energy in the morning to not be so sleepy. Thank you, Ms. Guillory.

Nobody in my school really knew of me until I started showing and it got out that I was pregnant for Olajawon. What started as me crying thinking my life was over and I could never make anything of myself now ended with me loving this little boy before I had ever met him. Though I was seventeen when I had my son I was still a teen mom. Being a teen parent and young mom was hard as hell let me tell you. You don't feel like a regular person because you aren't. You're a parent now regardless of your age and you have to act like a parent, at least that's what I thought.

My life was limited because I didn't really have the help or the knowledge I needed to be better. I figured it out. Part of everything I was in the early days was fake. I tried my best to be and act how I thought a mom would. So no more time for friends. During the years you're supposed to be figuring out yourself I was changing diapers, figuring out how to breastfeed, forcing a family together that shouldn't have been.

There's no time to think of what dress you're going to wear to prom. There are no more thoughts of what college I wanted to go to, there's just me, my baby, and my nanny.

I cried most days wondering how I got here. Thinking I wouldn't be enough for this little boy. Thinking about how I am going to make a family for him so he doesn't end up like me. I cried most days apologizing to him before he even blessed the earth because I didn't know how to be a mom. I didn't even have a mom so how was I going to do this? But as I looked at the women who held my hands and my legs and gave me words of encouragement. I knew that this little boy wouldn't care that I didn't have a mom. He only cared that I was his mom. After having my love, Isaiah Dawon Mason, this beautiful 7-pound baby boy and being left alone. I accepted that I would do this alone. Again nobody ever really said it but, nobody ever really helped either. I would look down on his cute little sleeping face and I would see the embodiment of my love. It was my Zai.

I thanked my mom in that hospital room after everyone left. Because I felt her hands on my face and I heard her voice telling me it would be ok and that I had it. My son came into this world not crying. Not because something was wrong but I honestly think because of her, Carla Ruth Gage.

Little did I know just how hard mothering would be. Ever since my mom died I had spent my life searching for somebody to love me. Wondering what was wrong with me that no one did. I spent so much time looking in the wrong places but I finally felt like I found it. In this little boy. With all of my missteps and crazy moods, it never swayed this little boy's love and acceptance of me. I worried every step of the way. I worried the first time he had a sinus infection as a baby. He was the happiest sick kid in the ER. I got scared the first time he fell off the bed. I cried thinking I hadn't even graduated. What am I going to do?

Six months later at eighteen, I graduated, not top of my class but not at the bottom of my class either. And guess who was right in the front cheering as his momma walked the stage to get her diploma? Isaiah Dawon Mason that's who. This girl who had struggled through so much. Who was still struggling through so much. My Zai was cheering for her because to him I was AMAZING. Just as my mom had been my everything, I was his. In that moment, in looking over at him I had never felt so close to my mom as I did then. She and I were part of the same club. The same love she'd felt for me I felt for him and nobody could take that. At that moment I decided I needed to heal, for him. He doesn't deserve a broken mom. BUT, what does that even mean?

After graduation, I went to Vista College in the daytime and worked at night. Though I absolutely HATED being a server the money was decent and needed. I eventually had to drop out of school during my internship and work full-time.

"I'm homesick all the time ... I just don't know where home is. There's this promise of happiness out there. I know it. I even feel it sometimes. But it's like chasing the moon - just when I think I have it, it disappears into the horizon.

- Sarah Addison Allen

Chapter VIII

I honestly didn't know how to start this chapter. I had to take a break from writing because with writing this one I had to think about and deal with things I thought I'd let die. But I hadn't, everything that messed me up was still there. None of it has suffocated in its respective boxes. I can sit and talk about it all day but I will never feel better or get over it. I guess that's why therapy didn't really work for me to move on.

When you really think about it, so much of you comes from your parents. How you carry yourself as a woman most of the time comes from your mom or whatever woman played a major part in your upbringing. As a young girl and later woman, what you accept from a man comes from your dad or whatever man played a major part in your upbringing. Now, because I didn't grow up with a mom or dad for that matter I didn't learn a lot that parents are supposed to teach you.

The only other man that was very instrumental in my life was my grandpa and he died within the same year as my mother. Now, I can lie and say that all that I am has come from movies I watched but it'd be just that, a lie. I have no clue where I learned some of the things I've accepted in life. Partly, from movies yes and I believe partly from my nanny. She taught me kindness and heart. But she never taught me boundaries.

Now I have this baby that's depending on me and needs me to be a grown up but I'm still a hurt kid, so what do I do? I play dress up, that's what.

Fake it till you make it right? I put all of my hopes and dreams into this precious little baby and vow to him that he won't be messed up like me. And you're probably asking yourself what exactly did I do? And the answer is, I became the mom I always wanted, I didn't want to miss a thing.

As a newborn, he spent most of his time with my nanny while I worked. I tried my damnedest to look past and work things out with his father so he could grow up in a two-parent household. Because kids that grow up in a two-parent household are happy kids, right?

Well, most of what I learned came from books, TV shows, and movies so yeah that's what made a happy healthy kid. Although it's been years, I still haven't dealt with losing my mom. But, I was somebody's mom now so my feelings were invalid compared to his.

During this time I wrote. Any and everything that popped into my mind I wrote down (5-star rating. Would 100% recommend). To the point I've had hundreds of notebooks that have had my thoughts on their pages, my tears too. Recently I was going through my things in storage and came across a ziplock bag of letters I wrote to Isaiah and other children I might have in the future.

I started doing that because I wished I had letters or even a note from my mom that I could read when I was feeling down or needed her words. So, I wrote my words down for him/them. ANYWAY, I came across one sheet of paper that wasn't a letter but my words all the same. Upon reading them I wondered why I would want to keep them so close to something that was so precious to me. Then I smiled, because I'm not that girl anymore. I'm not sure when I wrote it but I felt that girl's pain. Though I'm sure in the moment of writing those words I didn't feel relief, rereading them now I do. I wish to hug that girl, however old she was.

"My reality is one I hate.

My story is not yet finished, but this chapter is truly not one of interest to me. It is one of pure boredom, loneliness, anger and slight depression.

I have no clue how to be my own person. Even though I so badly want to be. That alone scares the hell out of me.

———My reality is one I hate———"

-Danielle M.

During my relationship with Isaiah's father, I started to smoke cigarettes and eventually black and milds, (a type of cigar). Lord was that boy stressful. (0-star rating. Would not recommend VERY addictive). He proposed and I said yes. Thinking I'm doing my duty to my son. Two-parent households are part of the vow I made to him so I'm going to follow through (I never did by the way. Thank God.) There was so much I needed to heal from but I didn't even know I needed to be healed. I always wondered "What's wrong with me? Why does nobody really want me? Why am I so broken?" Even though I had this thought I never thought, honey you need to grieve your mom and move on. After the destruction that was my relationship and being convinced nobody would want me or my baby, and that STILL feeling this pain I can't get rid of I decided to numb myself with sex yet again (5-star rating. Would recommend BUT not for the reason of numbing yourself. Also always be safe.) Honestly, I didn't even enjoy it half of the time. It wasn’t pleasurable and sometimes it hurt. But, I didn’t have to think about what was wrong with me. I didn’t have to be sad. Hell, I didn't have to feel any emotions. Just get my rocks off and keep it moving.

I never really had sex frivolously. I had a few partners over the years and just recycled simply because I’m a creature of habit and didn’t want to get to know new people. Though I always got checked regularly. Because the only way you can be sure you don’t have anything is to not have sex. I was always safe and used protection but I was a hypochondriac, I used to think anything meant I was dying or God was punishing me for fornicating before I was married. Through everything I journaled though. I also tried to keep a good relationship with God. But I was still pissed at him, and it would come in waves.

Like, one minute I'm talking to him and praying every day. The next minute I'm cursing his name and screaming at him for being so selfish and taking my mom. For not protecting me. For not thinking I needed her more. That would usually happen when I was already down. AGAIN not connecting the dots that all of my anger and resentment was coming from not actually grieving the loss of my mother. And let me tell you baby when you don't grieve and work through what you need to work through oh my Lord it makes you angry. All of that building up over YEARS, makes you want to just hurt people at times. Because shit I'm hurting so you're going to hurt too. I need you to feel my pain.

My my my, the universe, God, the higher being, whatever you want to call that entity has been patient with me. Because when I tell you that's exactly what I was on. Up until fairly recently I have been angry and lost. I have given them a run for their money and I'm sure there are some moments where they're scratching or shaking their head with me.

Over the years I've been angry. Most people have a medium, I call it the chill space. Where they're just content, I've never had that after my mom died. For some reason I only had feelings of rage and feelings of contentment; there was no medium for me, no peace. Unless I was looking at my son. When it was just me and Isaiah I didn't feel as numb. I thought this is what love for your child feels like. I wondered if this feeling was how my mom felt about my brother and me when she was alive. I began associating the unconditional love I had for Isaiah with the way love stories and romance movies made me feel: because that's like the same thing right? To this day that happiness still feels odd. It doesn't belong to me. Like I'm just borrowing it. But my family wasn't complete without a second parent, or that's what I thought. So that was my new goal: find him another parent. In order for my son to not turn out like me he needed two parents to love him. Though I loved women it needed to be a man. Somebody that could teach him how to be a man and they had to be stable. Even if I ended up unhappy it was ok as long as my son had stability and another parent.

Outside of my son, I didn't deal with feelings. I didn't know how to console others when they cried, that's actually something I still struggle with. I guess that's another way I coped through it; evading my feelings. Other than my son the only things that made me feel good were movies, shows, and music. But you shouldn't evade your feelings. Because they always come out eventually, for me that was usually anger. I set out to be the best mom I could be instead. But I had lost what family means. I knew the structure of what it needed but I didn't remember what family was. My family hadn't acted as a family in so long that I lost the memories of it. The only references I had were the books I'd read and movies. Not realistic BUT how'd I know?

I'd loved as much as I was capable of and it was accepted. I'd eventually found the perfect man to be a role model to my son. We'd dated for about five years before getting engaged and married. It'd seem like the logical thing to do, right? We rarely argued and had an understanding. He'd lead and I would follow, head of the family and all of that, you know? He decided to go to the military(such a headache). That's when I started to wonder if maybe I had separation issues. A year later we divorced. This happens in life and relationships fall apart. I don't deal with things well in case you've forgotten. And this whole time I've been falling back into a black hole. I would go through manic episodes that would last a few days sometimes. Then, I'd go through depression episodes and they'd last months.

Now through this, I've been thinking I was keeping Isaiah safe from that part of me. It never crossed my mind that he was growing up learning to deal with my moods; that maybe I need to heal myself for him and me. I just knew I had to keep him separate from that part of me. I'm so thankful to my nanny for helping me during the episodes of my depression. Without her, I wouldn't have been able to cope with being a new mother to this beautiful baby boy. I wouldn't have been able to give him what he needed to be healthy physically and emotionally. My nanny put me in therapy after my mom died, but it never helped, (5-star rating, would 100 percent recommend). Just because it didn't work for me doesn't mean it doesn't work. I really wish this was talked about more in black families, therapy is ok, and sometimes it's necessary. Do you know what worked for me though? Writing, I needed to physically get the words out of me. How I was feeling and what was going on. Sometimes I would even write letters to my mom. Part of me felt she could read the words if I wrote them down for her. Even though I found this new coping mechanism that worked for me, in times of high stress I would revert back to cutting. Then, I learned that as an adult you could walk into any hardware store or craft shop, hell even Walmart, and buy a pack of razor blades or a crafting blade. Nobody looked at you crazy because it was a normal thing people do. When I didn't know what to do and the feeling of being alone was almost crushing I'd revert back. But, let me say, just because you have a slip-up and you fall back into old habits does not mean you are a failure or a bad person. It doesn't mean you can't pull yourself out of it. It doesn't mean you can't get better. Even if you don't have family or a friend to help pull you out. There is something in your life that depends on you. Whether it's your cat or dog, or maybe it's your plants. Maybe there's a kid you're nice to when nobody else in their life is nice to them. SOMETHING or SOMEBODY depends on you living and being here.

My person was/is Isaiah. Even though I had a friend and cousin that would try to help. All they had to mention was him and I could pull myself out. I want him to remember me how I remember my mom. My son had become my anchor in this world. I was growing up with this kid even though I was his mother and NOBODY could mother him like I would.

Once I realized just how important I am to this little human I knew I had to fix myself. I still felt like I wasn't enough family for him. I would go back and forth with the thought until I just let it go. He was happy with me and all of my broken pieces. But, he deserves more than my broken pieces.

don't run away from heavy emotions, honor the anger, give pain the space it needs to breathe - this is how we let go

- yung pueblo

Chapter IX

After my mom died I developed insomnia, suicidal ideology, chronic depression, and chronic anxiety. Those are just fancy words to say I became a night owl, I would fantasize about my death, was overly sad without knowing why most of the time and the world made me really, really nervous. Now, I didn't put it that way to make it seem not real or not really important. It's just that people usually understand things better when you put them in words they understand. So there you go.

This worked out for me in a way, since I was my calmest when I was alone. Everybody's sleeping and the house is quiet. The downside is you're alone with your thoughts which sucked for me sometimes since I'm an overthinker. Also, when you're dating somebody that's very insecure you get accused of cheating a lot. Who knew (insert shoulder shrug here). Through the years I have tried yoga, meditation, burning incense, hell, and even nice long uninterrupted hot baths to no avail. I did learn however I'm not as bendy as I think I am. I don't have an "inner vision" or whatever you call it. I close my eyes and see the inside of my eyelids. Oh and, I don't really like incense. If these things work for you, kudos really.

Sometimes if you throw a bunch of things at the wall something is bound to stick (or something like that). I learned that music, art, and food bring me peace. I also learned that breaking stuff made me feel better 99 percent of the time, but who wants to break their own things right? I have an uncle, cool as a fan, who had wood pallets in his backyard. One day I was sitting with him at my aunt's house venting about whichever member of the male species had angered me at the time. His advice, "Go in the backyard and bust some of those pallets up, get some of that frustration out."

Oh me oh my, was I in heaven. At first, I looked at this man crazy because, what? But, I followed him out back nonetheless. He took one of the pallets off the stack then handed me a sledgehammer and I went to work. To say it was therapeutic would be putting this experience mildly. The weight of the sledgehammer in my hands as I swung it over my shoulder time and time again, pure bliss. And I actually felt better afterward. I would advise wearing protective gear. I didn't get hurt or anything, just safety first, ya know. That was one coping mechanism I used for my need to destroy things when I was upset. I hadn't yet learned how to use my words to describe what I was feeling. I didn't even know these things I was feeling had words.

Ok, let's pause for an educational moment. This comes from the Integrative Life Center:

"Children don't have the ability to understand

their role in complex issues. Therefore, trauma can lead to feelings of personal responsibility, lack of stability, feelings of shame or guilt, and a mistrust of those around them. These symptoms can occur in childhood and remain into adulthood.

Trauma during developmental years changes the way a child's brain develops, leading to issues in many areas of your life. You learn healthy emotional processing — attaching the correct emotional response to an external stimulus — in childhood. Childhood trauma can make forming these connections difficult. It makes it challenging for an adult to determine the appropriate response to experiences. Also, Childhood trauma can cause adults to have a difficult time managing stressful situations. As a result, it is common for people to turn to food, drugs, or alcohol as a coping mechanism."
Now throughout the years, I've felt like something is wrong with me. Because the facts

are something WAS wrong with me. I've been grieving for the last fifteen years. It's really been fifteen years y'all. I've always been treated like something broken that needed to be fixed. But, I wasn't broken, just sad and ignorant to the fact that that's okay. Hell there are sixty-year-olds that lose a parent and go into a depression. The difference is as an adult it's your responsibility to find the tools to navigate through those emotions and that empty space. As a child, you don't have those same responsibilities. Your brain isn't even developed so the way to digest what this even means let alone what the next steps are in getting through it, well it's nonexistent.

Now, back to this broken mess. I'd been treated like a broken toy for so long that I started to believe it. I'd been treated like an option or obligation over the course of fifteen years that I believed these people. That was actually further from the truth. Being ignorant to the fact of me not being broken I decided to teach myself to meditate and became knowledgeable in crystals and such.

I'm sure there are many people who would advise that I should've just prayed or something of that sort. But, that's a journey all on its own. For a long time, I've felt something has been wrong with me, and it was. BUT at the same time, I was overthinking everything. Eventually, I got to a point where I started to take accountability for myself. I started to get an understanding that the things that happened to me and how I grew up wasn't my fault but how I handled things moving forward was my responsibility.

I have to give so many thanks to my bonus mom Alice. She has walked with me through so much. I can't even remember when we reconnected but, I love that woman as if she birthed me herself. Alice has shown me that words matter so much. How you use them with yourself and with others. She's shown me that forgiveness is possible. Also, that you don't have to be blood to love. Alice, as you read this know, just how appreciative I am to have you in my life and, I know without a doubt my mom is happy you're in my life as well. I can't tell you the number of times I've called this woman to rant about something that's made me mad beyond words I know to say. The way she calms me and helps me think more clearly and rationally as nobody else can honestly. She is a patient, calm, and rational voice when I really need it. Even when I don't want to hear it. Even when I get upset with her and go all silent treatment like a child, once I've come back to my senses she welcomes me back with open arms as a mother should. Not once has she tried to overstep as my mom. She's always just been my Alice. Nothing more nothing less.

I don't know if she knows this but she taught me ways to cope. She told me something her mom told her and it's really stuck with me. She said, "When you need to cry, cry, but you only get five minutes. After your five minutes are up dry your tears pull yourself together and do what you got to do." (To clarify, she did not mean five minutes literally. Her point was to not dwell on the sadness.) I wish I could've met her mom, she sounded amazing. Alice also taught me it doesn't matter what age you are when you lose a parent. It still hurts just as deeply. She made me feel not as crazy for how I was feeling about my mom's death, not as alone. I'm a very firm believer in 'You can't really understand what a person is going through with certain things unless you yourself have been through it. There have been times when I will call her while I'm at work because it just hit me again and I get to missing my mom and she'd talk me through what it is I'm feeling. Telling me, "Okay, you have five minutes. After that, you have to go back to work, do what you have to do." Thank you Gigi, you have been so important in my growth.

It wasn't until the pandemic hit the world that things started to truly truly get into perspective for me. I really started to wonder, "Why are you this way?". It was just good timing that the world was at a standstill for the most part. TikTok has helped me so much in such a short period of time. There are so many therapists on that app giving insight into things I never thought of. I follow a few black therapists and their 15-60 second videos have been so helpful to my life.

I figured out I had suffered a traumatic experience. Also, that I'm not alone, there are so many people out in the world that have been through some really tough stuff. For many of them, just like myself it's just life. You get back up and keep moving forward. To stay still is to die (not literally but still). To be honest, learning that wasn't my reason for writing all of this down. My reason was because I'm a writer.

That's how I work through things. I need to physically get my pain out of me in some other kind of way. The unhealthy way was to self-harm (0 stars WOULD NOT RECOMMEND. STAY AWAY FROM THIS ONE). The healthy way I've learned is to write (5 stars). Also, I found out some information I didn't know before. Which made me look at all the details of my mom's death I thought I knew in a new perspective. Not the eyes of a scared and hurt girl but, the eyes of an evolving, healing, more aware woman.

I suffered alone. Stuff inside my head for many many years. I know now that I, just like you reading this, am not alone. Losing a parent is inevitable. The when is different for everybody. But you don't stop once they do. Keep going, it's getting better.

Note to self:

When things feel overwhelming, remember:

- One thought at a time
- One task at a time
- One day at a time

Chapter X

I wish I could say with confidence that I am healed. I'm not. It gets more and more tolerable but not necessarily better. I actually greatly dislike when people say that "it gets better". I mean what exactly gets better? Do you start to get over the fact that the person who cared the most for you In this world Is now gone? Does the color come back to the world like before? I mean I understand, you're just trying to make us feel better BUT I feel like I speak for all that have lost a parent they were close to.... It's not helpful at all. In some cases, It's better to say "I'm here If you need to talk. If you need somebody to talk to you can call me. If you need anything I'm here." And actually mean It, most people don't actually mean It, it's just something to say in order to fill the space.

Most people do this without meaning to or even know they're doing it. I can't speak for all but I personally rather you say nothing at all than just fill the space with words that you don't mean. Because some people need that extra help to pull them out of the darkness they might enter. If you're saying you'll be there and a person in need actually reaches out but you didn't really mean it or you have too much on your plate can sometimes do more harm than good.

I actually had to pause again while writing this. Just when I think I'm getting to a better place I spaz. I understand so much more that grief is an ocean. Meaning : it comes in waves ebbing and flowing. Sometimes the water is calm, and sometimes it is overwhelming. All we can do is learn to swim. At this beautiful age I am, I still don't know how to swim.

Imagine being at a birthday party. Sitting outside with your aunt and siblings telling stories and reminiscing about your deceased mother. The events of her death come up.

Imagine me learning that I'd been lied to about when and how she died; trying to hold myself together because I am most definitely at a kid's birthday party. Imagine looking over at my boyfriend who sees that I'm about to rip open at the seams. He shakes his head no and mouths "Not here", nobody else has caught on to the replay going on in my head or to the fact that I am so close to dissolving in a puddle of emotions. JUST as I start to get the cap back on my emotions, because there's a time and a place right? I have a feeling of déjà vu as my aunt starts what seems like a painfully slow walk towards you. To which I shake my head no because I've been here before. Different aunt but the feeling is the same and I know if I let her hug me my night is done. Again I shake my head pleading, "please, no". Tears are starting to fall. Right as I'm about to scream, "NO". My boyfriend (Kenneth you're the best for seeing this) pulls me to a corner of the backyard. "Pull it together", he says. "Not here. The kids will start to worry. Your son will start to worry." Knowing that to be true I swallow the rest of the tears that threaten to fall from my eyes. It takes me a minute but I pull it together. Seeing as that was NOT the place to have my five minutes.

Going back to our little huddle after some helpful words from a cousin. I learned the last time I told my mom "I love you.", that morning she died shortly after. I learned that the whole time I was at school that day and playing in the hospital hallway thinking my mom was coming home she was already brain-dead. She was put on ventilators because she was an organ donor. I never understood out-of-body experiences until that night. Because as I'm hearing these things from my aunt I'm not liking the woman standing across from me but, I'm looking down on all of it. I see my brother and sister shedding tears from above. I even see myself crying and I feel betrayed. I think to myself no my nanny wouldn't lie to us. She wouldn't have us think this one thing this whole time. I learned that I, in fact, wasn't abandoned by my aunt and granny. But, they were given the runaround when asked to see us or told we were busy. We continue this conversation with tears still in our eyes even as it comes to an end. Shuffling kids in cars and getting them home to be bathed and start bedtime routines. I can't stop replaying everything that was told to me. Days go by and I'm going back and forth on what to do. Do I confront the siblings of my mother? (Because I don't know who made the decision not to pull my brother and me out of school when it was learned that our mother died.) Do I let it just die since it's been years?

Finally, I decided to just ask. Entering a group chat with my aunt and nanny (mom's sisters) and my brother. I simply asked and it went like this:

Me: Who decided to wait to tell us our mom had died and why?

AS: I don't know. I was not in a good place. I don't know when you found out.

Me: We found out at a Halloween party …. She was dead hours before toots told us…. Everybody had us thinking she was going to be ok and she'd been dead for hrs

AS: Well Sweetie I'm sorry. But why are y'all discussing this now?

Bro: We didn't know anything. We just thought she passed at the hospital

AS: No she passed at home. They took her to the hospital because she was an organ donor.

Bro: And nobody told us that it's like it reopened a closed wound

AS: Ok I'm not sure why y'all are back

dooring all of this. But I don't linger on those things. When I look back I remember and talk about good times. So why go through the hurt again?

Me: Well obviously it doesn't matter to anybody but us. No need to linger on the past as you say. Have a great night auntie

Bro: I'm good 💪it just keeps coming up in my head from time to time

Me: Not that it matters but it pissed me off to hear that from somebody that didn't even raise me. I don't really care about the reason. I'm annoyed because I was lied to. That's the just. Idc that it's the past or whatever. You lost your sister and I lost my damned mother. And to find out from somebody else that she died AT HOME EARLIER THAT DAY…. But i guess it doesn't matter we were just kids right..
that's just old news.

And we never talked about it again. Not trusting the few who "raised" me I wanted to get a few other viewpoints from important people to me on my dad's side of my family; on the events that happened and how that affected them. Namely my dad and sister. It was beyond enlightening and informative. I decided to do it interview style. Since that was easiest for me. First up my sister.

Interviews

This is the part of my story where I talked to others. I talked to four people, three of whom were of no blood relation to my mom but were still impacted by her death. My sister Christina, my brother Nathen, my aunt Miracle, and my father Richard. Honestly, it was cathartic to hear them talk about their experience following her death. Here's what they had to say. (These are not put in an order.)

P.S. Some of these conversations go off on a tangent but I feel they are still important to the overall story. I wish I could add the actual audio to this story because talking to them and hearing the passions with which they spoke was a beautiful moment in itself. Thank you for sticking with me this far.

Chapter X I

My sister My sister. Even though we don't share a mom as well as a dad there's nothing half about you. My whole life you've always been my magical and mysterious big sister. I love that you loved my mom as much as I did. It fills my heart that she saw you as her kid as well and that you were around me growing up as long as you were. Thank you so much for taking the timc to talk about her with me.

CHRISTINA (MY SISTER)

"You make things so difficult for no reason, " I laugh. "OK, I actually wrote questions this time. Are you ready?"

"Yes"

"OK so first I want you to state your name and who you were to my mother?"

“My current name?"

“Any name, just pick one."

“My name is Christina. I'll just go by Christina. And, I think to your mother, I was a bonus daughter; a bonus kid, I would say. I would think so."

“OK, how did you find out that she died like that? Somebody call you? Or did you just like hear it through the Grapevine?"

“ I'm pretty sure my daddy told me. Umm, I honestly can't remember much about it aside from he’s the one that told me."

“Ok, do you remember how you felt after hearing that?"

“Um, I mostly felt sad for you and for

Nathan. And, just kind of, I don't know how to describe the feeling."

"Throw some words out there and see if they stick."

"There's like a — I guess like an empty spot. Umm, because I think the last time I saw your mom was when I came out here after graduation, I want to say."

"At Granny House."

"Yes, Yeah, I came out here. And so I just kind of remembered, I guess reminisced on the time that we spent together because she came and got me and we hung out and we chatted. You know, all that good stuff. So I just kind of reflected on the fact that the last time I saw her was good."

“You hung out with my mom? (Pause) without me.”

“Mmhm.”

“Just y’all two... doing stuff? Not gonna lie, Kinda jealous and don't know how to feel about it. Not gonna lie.”

“Yes, it was, It was nice. Yeah. She actually (laughs) doesn't know if anybody realizes it. Was it her? (Confusion) or was it Aunt Miracle? I don't know, I can't remember now. One of the two, I want to say it was her honestly. Is the one that took me to get my belly button pierced when I was out here. Got in some trouble about that when I got back to California.”

“Mischief.”

"But, we... We just kind of had a heart to heart, kind of conversation. Because I was 18 at that point. And, We just kinda chatted about all the things that, well not all the things, but some of the things that as a kid I didn't know or understand or you know had misconception of. Especially surrounding the dynamics of her, GiGi and my dad, you know. And she kind of cleared some things up for me. But it wasn't like... it was just normal. It was just a normal kind of conversation. And it was, it was almost like, she realized that I'm old enough to just have this conversation with now, you know? And it wasn't, I don't know. It wasn't weird. It was just that she didn't feel like a grown up in that moment, it was like we were Gal Pals kind of, you know,

"Gal Pals? You are so old." (Laugh)

"I know."

"Do you feel like her passing changed our relationship in any way? Or affected our relationship in any way?"

Umm. No, and I say that because I wasn't here, you know, if I were here, I'm sure there would have been something that maybe would have brought us closer if I was here. But because I wasn't, things just kind of remained the same. Uh. Yeah, I don't think it would have changed anything."

"OK, OK. Do you feel like our relationship would have been different if she were still alive, or relatively the same like how it is now?"

“Umm.Yes, (smiles) If all factors were the same like now and I even if I came back when I came back. I think things would be different. I think we would probably be closer. Because she is somebody that I would have a relationship with. Just, you know, based on our last conversation and based on what she was to me when I was living here as a kid."

“OK. Are there any words you wish you could say to her though?"

“Um. I don't know. That's a tough one. I just like to see her smile again, hear her laugh; see her around, our kids. knowing how much she loved kids."

“ I feel like she would be stressing me out."

“Yeah.”

“Do you have any stories or memories you like to share? That you would like to be in print.”

“ I don't know. Because honestly, like my childhood memories, the specifics are not that good and I don't know if it's because I bounced around so much. It was too much for my young mind to keep everything in order so I don’t have like Specific you know”

“That's OK. That's cool. Well that's all I got. That's all the questions I could think of. Is there anything else you want to say.”

Just Carla I Love you. I miss you. I wish you wouldn’t have done this. You made me cry.”

“AWW you want a hug? I'm very awkward with people crying and hugging , but I can give you a hug. You want to hug? I can do that. It's OK...(awkwardly pats on back and hold while crying)"

“I hate your hug. That’s the worst huh I’ve ever gotten."

“ I'm sorry. I'm sorry. I told you I was awkward so.. But I tried so A for effort"

Chapter X I . I

This lady here is my best friend. I know exactly what I will always get from her. Thank You Aunt Miracle for always respecting me enough, to be honest with me. You knew a different woman than I did. I am thankful you let me see her through your eyes.

AUNT MIRACLE (MY PATERNAL AUNT)

"OK. Weird dude. I know what I'm doing. OK, so.I probably should have written the questions down huh?"

"You don't have it in your notes."

"No."

"Ok So the first Question would be how did you find out that my mom was... bucket kicked?"

“Neicy called me”

“Like she just called you one day?”

“Well I told you I talked to your momma earlier that day or whatever. Then Niecy had called me and told me that she had passed away and she was in the hospital.”

“Ok, what were your initial thoughts, like the whole thought process of the whole thing?”

“That it was fucked up the way they did it… it was all fucked up. The way they did it. First of all, when we got there, I saw her, and they had her on the thing, keeping her alive. Well, she was a donor. But they wanted to make y'all think she was still alive and she really wasn't alive. You could tell she was gone because her tears dried up on her face."

"Hmm. ok, so how did you deal with everything from the time you found out up until funeral time? I think it was a two-week difference."

"Shit it hurt because that was like my sister, like we had just did I think mothers day because I remember crying to her and was telling her that Rob didn't get me anything for mothers day. And that's when she brung you and Nathan over. Do you remember that? She gave me a card and some money and I think something else she had bought me. I kinda felt bad because she had been asking me to take her to the mall but it's like I was working so much I just couldn't get there. But, she wanted to get to the mall so bad I just never knew why but when she passed I was like 'damn maybe she knew she was about to leave and that's what she wanted to, you know, do with me.' it was real fucked up when we went to the funeral because when I went to give yo aunty a hung she told me dont touch her. But I had talked to Kat and she basically told me don't worry about it. You know it's ok or whatever."

SIDENOTE "Wait, who is Kat?"

"Neicy ex-girlfriend Kat? You know who Kat is."

"OOOOH ms. Anne?"(I say with a confused look)

"No, I didn't say Anne. I said Kat. Let me

show you Kat press pause."

"No, it's fine. (I'm then shown a picture of a lady I don't remember and I say just that) I don't remember her."

"Yes you do, she used to have you all the time. It must have been that long since you've seen her."

"I remember Ms. Anne and the lady she was married to. Dang, now I don't remember the question I asked".

(Aunt Miracle reminds me of the question.)

"Ok so, I know you told me before it was shitty times after with trying to see us. Like how did that affect you is what I'm trying to ask."

“with your momma side of the family.

Yeah it pissed me off, because we was all family at first but then your moma died and it was like ‘Fuck me’ basically. So anytime I'd try to come get y'all or call yall it was always something. Like we could never get y'all or talk to yall. I don't know if maybe they thought I was going to get you and give you to your daddy. Which that didnt have shit to do with me. I didnt even fuck with him like that anyway."

“That shouldn't matter. Well I guess yes that does matter but it really shouldn't. Uum, what else, (at this moment my son decides to take this moment of me pausing to tell us he's bored and his cousins fell asleep. To which we remind him he can now watch whatever he wants and doesn't have to share the tv. He understood the assignment) (I then asked Aunt Miracle if she's cool with me quoting her or would she rather I leave certain things out. To which she says it's ok don't leave anything out."

"What's crazy is that the only people who didnt treat me any differently were Ada, Sherlette, Frank, Big Gary, Rachael. I didn't have any problems with them. When it came down to your aunties and popeye. I couldn't believe he even turned on me like that."

"I think it was just a lot, I think."

"ok but we were all family though. I mean I can understand that, we were all going through this together, we all lost a loved one. Shit I been knowing Carla since she used to watch me when I was asleep and talk to me when she thought I was dead. When Chris told her I was dead in the bed and she really thought I was dead."

"That's mean, what the hell... would you say that my mom was the glue of holding the two sides together?"

"It goes back to when I was little. hell yeah. When your momma was alive we had so many family functions. I used to go to family functions all the time. And it's crazy because your momma and daddy weren't even together anymore. That's how long your momma has been around me. I remember your aunty Rachael got married at Ma Peas house in the front room. I used to spend the night. You were born with six fingers on each hand. I remember the thing wrapped around your fingers and they fell off and your momma kept them in a jar (gross and weird I know) . I'm telling you that's how much your mom was in my life. Like if my mom punished me, I'M GOING STAY AT CARLA HOUSE OR IM GOING STAY AT MA PEAS AND THEM HOUSE.

So I would go to your momma house. I used to stay there so damned much. Ask nookie we used to be in that bitch so fucking much. Even when Frank made it to the NFL and bought that house on Lucas."

"How would you say that changed our relationship? Because we didn't talk anymore until after I graduated."

“I don't think it changed our relationship. We just weren't able to talk to each other like we wanted to. Like I wanted to talk to you go fucking bad and I know you did too because we was ALWAYS TOGETHER. Like yall was never not there and we just couldn't. Like yall was always there. So I just think when we finally started back talking to each other we just picked up where we left off. It was never nothing different."

“hhmm??? I don't know what else to ask. How do you think things would be different if she had not died? I know that's a HUGE what if. But What If?"

“if she had not died? I think things would be a whole lot different. Because yall never wanted to make yall momma unhappy. I dont think yall would have kids. I think all that came from yall wanting to find love and yall mom was gone. I think that's the way yall found love, yall was so young and she was gone. I think if she was still here she'd be at this table and we'd be playing that card game that she liked to play all the time. With her Dr. Pepper, and I would have to find nobody to braid my hair because she would have kept my hair braided."

"facts cats. I've actually thought about that too."

"I just dont think yall would've had it as bad. Things definitely would've been totally different. I'm not gonna lie sometimes I do sit around and wish like 'man i wish i still had my sister' it would be so much easier. Just to have her to talk to, she was always there."

"Yeah, she was a very blunt lady. She was a thug lol."

"I remember she let me use her car but she forgot to tell me that it doesn't start right off. Sometimes you have to jiggle it to get it going, so I'm stuck in the damned Walgreens parking lot. That's when she was working at Antioch daycare when it used to be off Washington Blvd, and i called her like 'aye yo car wont start.' she said 'yeah i forgot to tell you, you gotta keep turning the key' i said 'really, that's really what we gonna do Carla?"

"I almost ran into that daycare. Nathan and I were playing in the car. You know how kids are. WELL the car was actually on and Nathan dumb ass put it in gear. Like he was playing and bumped it some kinda way and put it in gear like he didnt mean too and man that car shot forward over that bump. Momma was like WHAT THE F.. and i'm like oh shit. I'm panicking and some kind of way Nathan got the car to stop. I'm sitting there crying like I'm sorry I'm sorry, crying and shit. I almost crashed two of her cars"

Chapter X I . II

My father and I have a very difficult relationship. But, it is as honest as it can be with us. I appreciate your honesty this day as well dad. It meant so much to me that you would agree to sit with me and talk about my mother (everything didn't make the cut) and answer a few questions I've wanted to ask surrounding the topic of Ms. Carla.

Richard (My Dad)

"So I called him. I say, 'Hey man, what's going on? This happened. I'm going to get my kids, man, what's my rights? He says, well how old are they?' I think I told him you were 12 or 13."

"Yeah, I had just turned 13 and Nathen was like 11."

"OK, I told him you were 12 and Nathen was 10. He said, 'Well, you ain't gonna like it, bro.' Something like that, but he said, 'You can get the boy, but you can't get the girl because in Texas law she's old enough to make a decision on her own as far as what she wants to stay. But you're not going to get either one of them because they're not gonna break up siblings. So, if she says she doesn't wanna go, they're not allowing either one to go with you, you know; they're not gonna force one of them to go with you.' So now I'm mad. So I'm driving home mad and stuff mad. At first I didn't even remember going to the funeral, but after you said something, I was like Oh yeah, yeah, yeah, I do remember being there. Because your family got mad. Because you were like 'I want my daddy.'"

"I didn't want to mess with anybody. If your name is not Richard, get out of my face."

"So all that goes down. And later on at night I went by pop house, this was when yall was living on Oriole. You were cool but Nathan had jumped out a window or something? They were like 'yeah he ran away.' or whatever."

"Yeah, I remember that. I forgot that he jumped out the window."

"My brain goes straight to this ain't nothing new, because of the way it was said. I knew that, that wasn't anything new; this is common. And that makes me think about something else but I digress. Then your uncle and your cousin try to put me on the little round table and stuff, man, blah, blah, this and blah, blah that. And, you know, she doesn't wanna go with you. You know, I have already worked on myself. So, I was prepared for certain things to transpire. I hear what you're saying and I understand where you're coming from. But, at the same time FUCK about what y'all saying to be honest with you." he laughs at this but continues,

"Because this is where I'm at, at the end of the day. My thought process is always, at the end of the day it doesn't matter whether you want it or not, or you know, you accept it or not; those are my fucking children. You know, regardless of how they act, regardless if they want me to be their dad or not, I don't care. They'll figure it out one day, but they still my fucking children. But anyway, they had their little piece. I was like alright man, since I already knew where I stood as far as legality goes and yall could feel like y'all got a "W" but you know, I'm already ahead of the game and stuff."

"OK, I have a quick question. So do you think it would have gone differently if your name was on our birth certificate?"

"I thought my name was on your birth certificate. It wasn't?"

" Nope, not on either of ours."

“It wouldn't have been different. It wouldn't have gone differently, at all. My lawyer never brought up a birth certificate. He never said anything about a birth certificate. It's important, but it's not important. You have a deceased parent. And you have a person, whether his name is on the birth certificate or not, that says I am the parent. That person has never denied paternity. So since paternity was never denied and there's paperwork for that then yeah, that's the parent. So when I'm going back to Maryland, my thought process is, ‘well, if you can't bring Mohammed to the mountain, you bring the mountain to Mohammed.’ So, I'm moving back to Texas. That's just it, You know, it's a whole lot sooner than my plans were, but that's where my kids are, so I gotta go back to Texas. And that was my plan. I moved back and then y'all left. So now I'm mad."

"Yeah, that's what my next question is for you. How did you feel after hearing, 'I want to stay' then you got here and we were gone?"

"Oh I was mad. I was so Fucking mad."

"I realized I had never I've never lived with Nathen after mom died. After we talked to you, Me and Nathen never lived in the same house again. Ever until I graduated."

"Really, I didn't know that part. The fact that when I came back y'all was gone. I was like, they fucking did it anyway, you know. My boy tells me the courts are never going to separate them, and the family separates them anyway."

"It was a whole lot of letting children make decisions they should not have been making."

"Right! Right, right."

"Because it wasn't anything that was in the best interest of us, like it wasn't good for us to be where we were. I was just like, 'I want to stay here now', and it was just like OK."

"You and I had a talk one time and you were small. You were still a teenager at the time."

"Aww yes, the rebel years," I say this endearingly.

"Yeah, I think you were a teenager at the time that we were talking about this stuff. We were talking about decision making and you said that your family says that you're young but you make good decisions. At the time, I know you probably hated my guts when I said this. I was like, 'I understand what you're saying, baby, but you're way too young. You don't have enough tools in your toolbox to make the decisions that you're making.'"

"Ugh, and I hate that saying so much. Thanks so much. It pops into my head so randomly and I like, 'where the hell did this come from?'"

"And you know, people that don't have a vested interest in your real well-being will allow certain things you know. A real parent would not allow certain things regardless of how "good of a decision" they might think you have. And if 10 years down the road something changes, you know what happens. I make different decisions, you know I change. But for whatever's happening right now, I gotta make the best decision. I got to look at what's going on and make the best decision about what's happening. Period. But women, they pause life almost and try to fix whatever's going on. You know, what I like about me is that yeah, it's going on. Yes, it's fucked up. Yeah, you hurting? But you know what? When you wake up, you still gotta keep moving. You still gotta keep moving forward. You know what I'm saying. Oh. I don't know if this is going to get fixed. I don't know if it's always gonna be like this. Never know if it's gonna get resolved. But you have to keep moving forward. You can't sit in this spot and wait for something to happen over here. You gotta keep moving forward. You gotta keep trying to advance and get better. You know, I'm saying so."

"At almost 30, I'm only JUST starting to understand that. I only just realized that I have a tendency to do that. It's like the world stops. Like everything is just bigger than what it actually is. And I feel like If I don't fix this thing that's wrong, nothing 's gonna be right."

"When you get older, what you realize is that thing that you think is so big, it's so small compared to the rest of the ecosystem within your life. When I came back, thinking about it and letting it marinate in my head and stuff. I was kind of glad. Not glad that y'all didn't come with me, but that y'all wasn't forced to come with me. I was glad of that aspect of it because what would have happened was, y'all would have been resentful. All I wanted to do was show y'all a different life and wanted to show y'all black upwardly mobile black folks making real money doing real things. And y'all wouldn't have been able to see that because you would have been resentful. I'm saying you would have been thinking, 'well, that's my family over there, I don't know this dude and I don't want to be around here.' And now, instead of learning this whole new world, y'all bucking the system and now y'all becoming really rebellious as opposed to that minor rebellious thing that children go through as teenagers, it would have been amplified"

"So do you have any regrets, like returning to Texas earlier than you had planned"

"No, and one of the reasons I really don't have that type of regret, because I really don't live in regret per se, but we don't control how things flow. We don't have any real gauge like, 'ok this gonna happen at this time', but if it doesn't happen the way I want it to happen, I'm OK with flexing and molding myself within the confines of how things are going down now, because that's part of life. Life changes and it's not changing based on what you want it to be. It's changing based on what life is, you know? So the flower grows at its own pace. Grass grows at its own pace."

"Aww, that's cute. Look at you."

"Aye, chill, I'm a bad man. Don't let these pretty eyes fool you."

"Oh Lord. (insert dramatic eye roll) give a man a compliment and it goes straight to his head."

"That was my mindset at that time, you gotta roll with the punches. And let's say it's a situation like, I could've come back, y'all disbanded and I pushed pause and I just waited, wadling in my self-pity of 'whys' and 'how comes' and 'what should haves'. Where am I now? That would have stifled me for, what, another five or ten years at least. You gotta keep moving forward. It's not that you forget or don't acknowledge. You acknowledge even if you just only acknowledge it to yourself. Which is what I do. I beat myself up internally. You don't dismiss it or anything like that, but you have to keep moving forward. Because when they come back, If they come back, you don't want to be in the same place you were. Cause that's no growth at all. You wanna be somewhere. So if nothing else, at minimum, what they see is he's not in the same place. Whether or not they acknowledge it at the time. At some point on their journey through life they're gonna see 'oh, we showed up at this point then left and came back and he was in a different place'. And now ten years down the road you look back and say, ‘oh, I see he had a little growth from that point to that point. I wonder what that means’. Now you could do self-reflection on yourself and be like, ‘What does that say about me and where am I at? What should I be doing? And my growing’?"

“Did you have faith that your children would come to you, I guess”?

“Faith, did I have faith? That they would return. I don't know if I would say faith. I have faith in a lot of stuff, you know. But, I don't think I would use that word. Faith is almost like an anticipation of knowing that that thing would happen or confidence that that thing would happen. What I do know is, I will continue to put myself in position to be open and receptive to whatever happens. Regardless of how it shows up regardless of what goes down, however it happens. I'm open and receptive to that, positive or negative.

“If it was possible to do things differently, would you?"

“No. I do ponder that from time to time. But I would not change anything only because it would change who I am and it would change my growth. Now, who's to say I would have grown quicker if things had been different? You know, I'm saying, I don't know and I wouldn’t want to take that chance. I think my growth is good."

“Do you feel like we have a good relationship?

“No, I don't think so. Although that's

subjective. Who determines what is or isn't a "good relationship".

I don't think it's anyone's fault, it's just the way that it is.

I'm your father period, ain't nothing you can do about it. But, I think and move the way I do based on what I know and what I see and have seen. You're My Daughter period, ain't nothing you can do about that. I "Think" there's a lot you're still dealing with, I'm ok with being wrong.

A good relationship starts with a good foundation. We never had that, speaking to you as a child. I don't think you trust me, blindly, to know that I know what I'm talking about. You see, I understand who my Father is, where he comes from and all that right. He did not raise me, we are where we're at because of me. And I trust him blindly. If I ask a question and he gives me an answer I have a choice to follow or do what I wanna do. I have watched him and learned enough in life that I know I can trust what he says. I wasn't always there though.

But, when I wanna know something I have to ask because I ain't a kid no more and he understands that grown folks sometimes wanna do things their way, even if it's wrong or the long way.

I see so much of me in y'all, i.e. want to make it hard, till it hurts. But, I gotta bite my tongue and let y'all bump y'all's head till y'all say "Hey Pops what do you think about this?" And say have you tried this? And that's it, and keep it moving.

I can see the gift in all y'all but y'all refuse to tap in.

Bottom line, sometimes to build a relationship you gotta get outta your own way."

"Can you say at any point that you've been proud of the person I've become?"

"Yes, I can see myself being proud of the person you are becoming. The problem is where you're at now in your life you move forward then stop, for no reason I can see. Then you move forward some more then turn around then turn around again and start moving some moore. I think you don't believe in yourself enough to know that even if you can't see the floor you know it's there so you walk with confidence. Sometimes it seems like you're testing to make sure something is solid for you to step on to. I understand the "why" but it's hard to watch sometimes.

This book thing has shown me a different depth in you, which I am proud of. Parents always see moore in their children than their children see in themselves.

Everybody fails. Those that don't, don't try."

Chapter X I . III

This particular interview is very special to me. This is the first time my brother and I have sat down and had a talk about how we felt and what was going through our minds during this time in our lives. This is the only biological sibling I have from my mother and our relationship is totally different from that of my other siblings. This conversation was all love and honesty. Thank you Nathan.

NATHAN (MY BROTHER)

"I recorded it at this moment."

"OK. So how long is it gonna take?"

"As long as it takes, let's go. Ok, so for the purpose of the book. State your name and your relationship to my mother."

"Nathan Moore and I'm the first and only son."

"She has other sons, you're not the only one."

"I am the original player. Player one that's me."

"Alright, Morio headass."

"OK, this is kind of a stupid question because it's the same thing for me, but how did you find out that Mama died?"

"At the hospital. I remember them taking us to a back room and then Toots coming out then the doctor coming out. Toots pulled us to the side because he started talking to my grandpa. Then, Toots came to grab our hands. I remember what I was eating that day too."

"I didn't ask you all that' I just asked you how you found out."

"Well I'm giving details. You asked for my point of view and I'm telling my point of view. Now stop interrupting, you are being very rude. I had a bag of Doritos, it was when the sweet and spicy Doritos first came out, the purple bag; I also had a Sprite from the machine. Then, Toots said 'Baby I'm sorry yall momma gone.' That's what happened from my point of view."

"OK, uh. How do you feel like that changed our relationship?"

"Relationship between who?"

"Me and you. *insert eyeroll* I did say, "our."

"I thought you said overall. At first I didn't like you. I did not like you at all. You were more of a burden to me.. But then, you know, overtime, I started liking you... You were cool. I thought we got closer. We were separated for a long time. Then, we got back together. I feel like we've gotten a lot closer now, we kind of understand each other a little better."

"In what way did she feel like a burden?"

"Ohh, before my momma passed Danielle was a burden.. She got to sit in the front seat."

"We're talking about her being dead. You could've said deceased. You could've said she's laid down. She's with Jesus."

"Ok, I don't know. These questions are kind of hard for you. How did you feel after? Let's say from when they told us up until her funeral, how did you feel or do you remember how you felt or remember anything around that time?"

"Like in a mental state? Ohh. I remember everything. I was hurting. I was like 'damn, who's going to take care of me?' you know. I didn't know how it was going to go. Because, nobody could imagine losing a mom. At the end of the day, you only get one mom. So with her being gone I just didn't know what to do."

"Do you feel like our relationship would

have been different if she was still alive?"

"Yes."

"How so? Elaborate, my guy."

"I don't feel like we would have the connection that we have. I feel like we would just be like 'oh that's my sister, oh that's my brother'. But, because we don't have her we know that we all we got."

"Do you realize that we never lived together after mom died? I think we lived together for like 6 months. Maybe."

"I moved in with you for like two months."

"But we weren't living together. I left. I

was living in Pasadena."

"OK, I spent the night for 60 days. lol"

"You get on my nerves. no, but for real, we were separated."

"I was talking to your father and he was saying how Popeye and nanny gave him so much shit or whatever because they didn't want to split us up and the lawyer he talked to was basically like, I had to make the decision, so if I said I want to stay, then we stay. If I say I want to go, then you know that's a whole different thing."

"You made an executive decision, I just wanted to let you know that."

"Listen to what I say! But, his words are that he didn't fight because it was a lose-lose situation. Because they weren't gonna split us up or whatever. Then, he was pissed because they made such a big thing about not wanting to split us up and all this shit just to turn around and split us up literally a few months after all that happened. And I was like I never knew that. Did you?"

"Yeah I knew that. That's the day I jumped out the window and she explained that to me."

"Because when he came to the house Toots told me that he wanted us and told me 'Baby y'all about to have to go.'"

"So they told him that you jumped out the window. Because that's the night I told him I wanted to stay. I didn't know you were gone. He was like when he came over he talked to me and I guess he was asking where he was and Popeye or Toots told him that you jumped out the window. He was like, 'I knew that wasn't the first time that shit that was a thing.' I guess they were so calm about the situation. They weren't like 'Oh my God, we don't know where he is.' they were just like 'mmmm, he jumped out the window.'" *shoulder shrug*

"If you would've met me at that time I did not care... At 3 o'clock in the morning I'm walking to the store. Why? Because I want a snack."

"We really used to just be walking the streets at all hours of the night. Just out there. But, it's the Westend cops don't care. They're not really stopping people like they do now I guess. I didn't know any of that. About you jumping out the window, that they had told you, you know, because they never told me anything really, they just like, 'your daddy wanna talk to you, or whatever and it's really your decision'. I was just like, well, I can't leave my fucking brother, like I have to stay."

"Then I got in trouble one day and Toots kept reminding me that whole summer that I forgot all about. You know we're riding our bikes. Me, Dal, and Kamin up in the canal and all kinds of shit bro. Like we were having a good time for the whole summer. It came down to the last day and then she was like, 'you got your stuff together and packed Rachael coming to get you. And I'm like 'Yo, I got school.'"

"They didn't tell me anything. I just came home and he was gone. I forgot all about that. I just came home from school and then it was gone and I think I asked where he was , maybe way later in the day or something. They were like 'oh, he's staying with Rachael now. I was just like, OK, I didn't think anything, you know, that's crazy."

(Kenneth) "So dysfunctional, your family is very dysfunctional."

"And I never saw my brother again."

(Kenneth) "That's crazy he didn't even think to call you or nothing."

"We talked on Facebook and stuff like

that."

“But like, literally, we never saw each other, or even really talked to each other again, like deadness. Til we was damn near grown"

“It was never like, ‘I want to call my sister. See what my sister is doing.’ it was just like, you know, if I see her on facebook like , ‘Oh, Danielle on facebook whatsup.’"

(Kenneth) “I’m talking about when you knew you were about to leave. I'm surprised you didn't reach out then."

“Well we were like rivals, or arch nemesis"

(Kennenth) “At that point you should've thought like aye I’m losing my nemesis."

"Lol it wasn't like that though. It was like she was way over there. I'm way over here. I can FINALLY live my fucking life."

"Same for me like there's nobody to tell on me. I can do what I want to do."

(Kenneth) "Now ya'll older and y'all like 'where is my sister at? Where is my brother at?'"

"I think he was living with our dad and they got into a fight. He calls me like,' Man, this nigga put his hands on me and he trynna fight me.' I think I had just got out of school. I'm waiting to get picked up and I'm just like what do you want me to do? I can't fight no grown ass man. Then the phone falls or something."

"Bro around this time I was undefeated,

I wasn't going for none of that. This is how the fight with him and me started: So I'm at my granny house, right? Granny kept saying, 'I'm going to tell your daddy, I'm going to tell your daddy.' So around this time I was hot, heated, bro. I didn't give a fuck about anything. I'm like, 'I'm not scared of him.' I guess she went to the other room and called him. He pulls up, He's like, 'come on.' We go outside. He wants me to say yes, Sir. I'm yeah, yeah. Like I'm not scared of you, bro. I told him straight up. So he tries to grab me; so I grab him back like whatsup bro. I was in eighth grade you know around this time puberty really hitting hard; you playing sports hitting the weights. It's like bro, when I'm in my prime, but I'm just starting to lift. So we trying to throw each other around. Granny comes outside and says, 'Stop. Stop. Don't lose your life.' Granny gives me this speech and she says I'll be lucky to see past 25 and all kinds of stuff. I'm like man, I'm not tryna hear none of that stuff. Then we got back to Debra's house. So he's on the phone going off. That's when I called Danielle and he took the phone and told her he was going to call her back. Tryna talk smoothly to Danielle. Danielle was like 'What are you doing to my brother?!'"

"The people around me were looking at me like I was crazy, I was screaming on the phone, then he hung up on me."

"So I'm at the house and my step sister Kiara is there around this time too. She was like, 'what you doing?' I said, 'I'm about to leave.' she say, 'Well , do what you want to do.`` I go, 'Thanks, bye.' I had this big suitcase on wheels. So perfect for going down the street. I hopped over that back fence and was gone. They stayed around the corner from there. Start rolling my bag. Knock on the door, Danielle opens it... pregnant. I'm like, 'what?' I walked in the house, at the time she was with Lij, I walked in the living room and dude sitting on the couch playing the game WITH THE HEADSET! So I go into Toots ' room, she looks at me, she says, 'I don't have nowhere for you to go. I don't have anywhere for you to go. Then I tell her the story of everything that happens and she tells me to go put my bags down. Funniest thing. See bro, Danielle was going into labor. She was sitting on a pillow with a grapefruit. She starts crying. I say Danielle, what are you crying for? What's wrong, what's wrong? She goes, 'I can't peel my grapefruit.' I'm like what is that to cry for. I get the grapefruit from her to peel. Then she takes a deep breath and tells me to go get nanny. So I go wake Toots up. Her room is pitch black, no TV all you hear is the fan. I said Toots, Danielle says it's time, get the bag. She goes Aww he'll wake Charlie. So I go to Charlotte's room and say, 'It's time. We have to go to the hospital.'"

"I was just messing up everybody's night. While they were doing all this I called Sheyle to ask how labor felt. She told me to get off the phone with her and go tell my nanny. All that and they forgot everything that was important. Everything that was important."

(Kenneth) "He was excited. How can you get mad at him? I'd have forgotten something too if I was excited."

"Lost everything when I saw Isaiah. I mean I'm bawlin."

"He kept saying, ' It's so beautiful. It's so beautiful.' I'm just like 'what are you crying for?' he goes, 'I just. I just wish mom and pop was here to see this.' And I'm like get him outta here 'cause did you just have a baby? Then my baby daddy goes, 'Yeah, So I have a calculus test tomorrow. So I'm going to school in the morning.' I'm like, 'I think your Calc teacher will understand if you missed it. (he wasn't a supreme student to begin with) And he left promptly at 6:00 in the morning to go to school. It's funny to think back on that now. Because he was literally just in the room he didn't assist in anything. My best friend and nanny held my hands and helped me with breathing through labor. Yeah. Fun times back on subject. Please. We're not going down my ship. I don't."

"I thought it was all about you."

"No, Right now it's about you. It's not about me. OK? I'm just gonna omit his section."

"Oh, go ahead. My bad."

"I forgot the dang questions. Do you think your life would be different if your mother was still alive? In what way?"

“Yes. I wouldn't be an angry beaver all the time. I know I wouldn’t have as many kids. I know that for a fact. I feel like. I would have taken sports a lot more seriously. I would have had real moral support. It's a hurt feeling looking up in the stands and you see all your friends, family and stuff like that, and neither one of your parents are there for you."

“Are there any words you wish you could say to her now?"

“I would tell her I appreciate her because I think the way I am with kids is because of her. With her working at the daycare I always saw her taking care of somebody's kids. She was always raising somebody's kids."

Conclusion of Interviews

So, you might be asking why I don't have any interviews with any of my mom's brothers and/or sisters. The answer is very simple. That side of my family has shown me time and time again that they can not be honest with me when the subject of my mom comes up.

Also, I've worked really really hard to begin the process of moving on with my life and forgiving those who have wronged me BUT I am not there yet. I understand you forgive others for yourself not them but at this time I'm not in a place to not be affected when I'm lied to my face.

The interviews I did have were wonderful and I really do appreciate each and every person that speaks with me about my mom. I have very few memories of her so it warms me to hear the stories of others and see others smile and laugh when telling those stories and remembering her.

Chapter X II

Excerpt from baby photo diary: written by my mom…

Date: January 5, 1994

Place: St. Elizabeth Hospital

Occasion: Three days old. Baby first picture.

Date of birth January 2, 1994; 8lbs 4oz.

Red birthmark at the back of neck.

March, 1994

Place: Sears

Occasion: Three mos. Old picture. Wouldn't smile but you did yawn alot.

Smile

●

Date: May 26, 1994

Place: Olan Mills

Occasion: Danielle needed an updated picture. Gave everyone a hard time. Did not want to smile at all.

Excerpt from baby photo diary: written by me...

Date: September 8, 2006

Place: 1235 Bolivar(home for now)

Occasion: It's me Danielle. I'm 12 yrs old and cute as a button. Not a baby anymore, more like a young lady trying to find my way. I go to South Park junior high school, kinda cool. I still think I'm the stuff and mom has to knock me down sometimes. Also need to update a picture.

Date: September 29, 2020

Place: China, Texas

Occasion: Danielle is 26 now and still trying to find her way. I found an amazing friend.

I have a son now, he's 8. Life isn't great all the time but I promise to keep pushing. I am going to be great

---

These are some things I wrote to my mom:

10/28/2023

Dear Mom,

Almost a year has passed since I last wrote to you last. I can't put into words how I miss you. Some days feel so dull, like life isn't even real while others feel perfect just for a moment. Sometimes I feel like I'm just visiting but can't go back home. Kenneth helps with that sometimes. I really hate this family you left me with except for nanny toots. Did you ever feel like this? Did you ever feel like you didn't belong in this family; in this world? Why can't I tell my brother I love him? Why is that so hard to do? It's like if i dont tell him then he won't leave like everyone else. Or it won't hurt as much when he does. Stupid I know. Why do I deal with that man you decided to have kids with? I have so many questions you couldn't answer even if you were here. These are questions i have to answer myself

I'm writing a book, mom. I think it will help a lot of women who've lost a parental figure.

Well that's all for now. I love you momma.

Chapter X III

"I will always be here for you, I won't let you down or stand alone in this crazy world we live in. If you ever do start to feel down, out of place or alone just know i'm right here and always will be… I love you silly goose."

-Kenneth Parker

These words were written by the love of my life and I truly feel he means them. I'm not sure when this will come out but at the time that I'm writing this we've been together for almost two years. When I say this man loves me loud and unapologetically he really does, and makes sure I understand that I'm not alone. If I don't have anybody else I have him in my corner.

I know I don't make it easy at times but he sticks with me. Though we grew up differently he continues to give me grace and I'm learning to continue to give grace as well. I used to think healing could be done in a week; a month tops, but that's nowhere near true. I am healing everyday. As long as I choose everyday to continue and you should remember that too. Grief and healing is like the ocean. They come in waves; sometimes those waves of grief come in full force and flow over you something serious, BUT sometimes those healing waves push that grief out and you can breathe for a while. Healing is a life long process I think.

Just when I'm feeling overwhelmed by the waves in my ocean Kenneth, Isaiah and even GiGi are like floaters, a raft, or a helping hand. They keep me from drowning more often than I think they realize. Isaiah is my reminder to keep moving forward because he doesn't deserve a mom that's constantly drowning and on the verge of breaking. Gigi is an ear when I need it. She understands what it is I'm feeling. Though she lost her mom later in life than I did she understands it is such a struggle at times and she will listen.

Mr. Kenneth is so much I could write a book on just him. Kenneth chooses to love me everyday he walks this earth. He shows me that I am worthy just as I am. Worthy of being loved by another person. Worthy of being understood no matter where I am in my journey. Kenneth is part of my peace; a good man in a storm. He is calm when I am not and listens to my rants at 2 in the morning when I need to get it out. When I feel wrong and don't know how to explain it he holds me until I'm right again. I love you all so very much and will never forget what you mean to me.

There are still moments where I feel like I'm drowning. There are moments when I wish I could call my mom or go see her. Where I want to ask her for guidance and insight in parenting and just with life. I still very much struggle everyday with feeling loss and grief. But, I'm seeing the bigger picture; that I have to keep going. I have to continue for my son, for myself, and for my family.

I'm finally starting to form a little village around me and it is a beautiful thing to witness and be a part of. One of my biggest dilemmas is remembering I can most definitely ask for help, and it's ok to ask for help. It doesn't make me less than anybody else. It won't make you any less either. You aren't weak because you need help. You weren't made to handle everything alone. You weren't sculpted as you are to let life beat your tail. STAND UP! KEEP MOVING! Even if it feels like you aren't moving much, at least you are moving. Don't be still and stagnant for too long, love.

Navigating life after being left behind too soon can be more than difficult, and we might be wondering 'why me? Why does God hate me so much?', I promise you are not hated. You continue to stand tall in the midst of adversity and never give up. Form a dream or a goal and work towards it. Also continue to see the positive where you can.

I speak from experience that when you let darkness, negativity and depression settle and make a home in you it is so tough to get it out. It's so hard to let hatred and disdain go to the point it becomes a second skin.

You are loved. You are needed, even if you feel like nobody would notice if you were gone trust me they will. There is somebody in this world that has encountered you and never forgotten you. There would be a hole in someone's life if you no longer walked the earth. Remember as long as you don't give up, life gets bearable. It can't rain forever love.

"If you can't fly, then run. If you can't run, then walk. If you can't walk, then crawl, but whatever you do, you have to keep moving."

- Martin Luther King Jr.

Thank you

I would like to take this time to give a special Thank You for being in my corner from the very start of this. Not once did you second guess that I could do this and thank you.

Also, Thank You to the interviewees for taking the time to talk to me about my mother. Miracle Culbert, Nathen Moore, Christina Carter, and Richard Moore, You guys rock!

I really hope this has been as helpful to you reading this as it was for me writing it. I've learned so much about myself during this time and I'm so happy I kept going even when I felt like stopping. Thank you for your time.

Happy Healing!

Danielle Moore, born on January 2, 1994, in Beaumont, Texas, found solace and expression through the written word.

Her journey as a writer has been deeply influenced by her life experiences, including the joy of motherhood. Danielle is the proud mother of her beloved son, Isaiah Dawon Mason, whose presence in her life continues to inspire and motivate her creative endeavors.

With a heart fueled by love and a pen guided by sincerity, Danielle's writing resonates with authenticity and depth. Through her words, she explores the complexities of life, love, and loss, inviting readers to embark on transformative journeys of self-discovery and understanding.

Danielle Moore's debut book, 'The Daughter Left Behind: Navigating Life Without My Mother,' is a testament to her unwavering commitment to storytelling and her profound ability to touch the hearts of others. As she continues to pursue her passion for writing, Danielle remains dedicated to sharing her experiences and insights with the world, one page at a time.

www.ingramcontent.com/pod-product-compliance
Lightning Source LLC
LaVergne TN
LVHW050535100826
845148LV00002B/566